& LIFE
GOES ON

& LIFE
GOES ON

Lizanne Dyer

& LIFE GOES ON

iUniverse books may be ordered through booksellers or by contacting:

iUniverse
1663 Liberty Drive
Bloomington, IN 47403
www.iuniverse.com
1-800-Authors (1-800-288-4677)

Because of the dynamic nature of the Internet, any web addresses or links contained in this book may have changed since publication and may no longer be valid. The views expressed in this work are solely those of the author and do not necessarily reflect the views of the publisher, and the publisher hereby disclaims any responsibility for them.

Any people depicted in stock imagery provided by Getty Images are models, and such images are being used for illustrative purposes only. Certain stock imagery © Getty Images.

ISBN: 978-1-5320-7294-9 (sc)
ISBN: 978-1-5320-7293-2 (e)

Library of Congress Control Number: 2019905055

Print information available on the last page.

iUniverse rev. date: 04/26/2019

Dedication

Self-Healing Proclamation

No more New Year's resolutions,
Just self-healing proclamations.
It's time to put into action,
All the things I just continue to mention.

The work starts now, and it starts with me.
I'm determined to be all that I can be.
A change is coming, just wait and see;
From all my restraints I now set myself free.

There's potential in me that I'm willing to explore.
Each time I feel myself slipping, I'll just push a little more.
I can't imagine what all these years I've been waiting for;
Success stands within my reach, just beyond the "doubting door".

I deserve to be happy and I deserve the best.
Now is the time for me to put myself to the test.
I must remain focused and not worry about the stress.
When I finally reach my goal, there'll be lots of time to rest.

So no more New Year's resolutions,
That we break once we have the option.
Today I make the proclamation,
That true self-healing is my intention.

Many years ago, I read the phenomenal book "On Death and Dying" by American psychiatrist Elisabeth Kubler-Ross. In this profound piece of work, she highlighted, what she referred to as *the five stages of grief:* denial, anger, bargaining, depression and acceptance. According to Kubler-Ross, these are the stages that one goes through in dealing with grief, usually after the loss of a loved one.

As I struggled through my life, I came to realize that these five stages need not refer only to death. I found myself going through many of these stages. Not always in the specific order, and very often doubling back on a particular stage. Maybe I had died inside and was, in my own way, attempting to cope with the loss of my identity.

Identity; a crazy word, as for a long time I wasn't sure if I had one. I was whomever the situation required me to be. Daughter, teacher, counselor, confidant, lover; whatever the situation called for, I'd don my cap and be ready. Try to imagine suffering from Dissociative Identity Disorder: for each new situation, a new alter ego would show itself to help you cope. It got to the stage where I was uncertain of my personal likes and dislikes.

Now, I don't want it to seem that I grew up in what might be termed a "bad" family. That is quite the opposite. My family was one that didn't need a special occasion to come together and celebrate. The simple fact that it was Saturday, was reason enough to get the family together. The problem was, I never felt truly connected to any of it or them. I was the outsider looking in. I heard the laughter, saw the fun, but I just could not bring myself to be a part of it. It would take me many years to find out that this was simply a personality issue that I was dealing with, and did not necessarily have anything to do with them not wanting to include me. I guess you could say it was all in my mind. Nevertheless, this created some tension, which, to this day I still deal with.

Why did I choose to write this book? For the first part, writing has always been my escape. It is the place I can go to where nothing and no one can invade my thoughts. It took me a long time to open up and allow anyone to read any of my material. It made me feel so vulnerable. That one safe space was being invaded by another human being. I felt naked, judged. But I came to realize that in life, there will always be that one person who makes you feel that it's alright to be vulnerable, it means that you're human. To my sweet and loving rescuer, I say thank you. You may never fully understand how much you've helped me.

I am also able to share this now, because I believe that I might be at stage five in Kubler-Ross' list; acceptance. I have spent many years fighting my demons; some of which I've conquered and others that I continue to battle with. In spite of this, I think I'm at a place in my life where I can accept myself for who I am without the need for external validation. My struggles are what made me who I am today. I'm a stronger person because of them.

Through the use of my poems. I hope to take you through my stages of "grief", and just maybe, someone out there would find solace in what I have written and see that it's not a dead end tunnel. There's an opening at the other end where there is peace and joy, and all those things you've been searching for all your life. It's just a matter of staying the course and pushing through, no matter how difficult it may get at times.

I still struggle at times, but now my demons know who is in charge.

<u>DENIAL</u>

This could not be real. I had to be dreaming. After everything I'd been through, God had chosen this moment to take away one of the greatest sources of stability in my life. I had held it together until then, but I truly believe this is when things really began to spiral out of control for me. My sweet "Grams" was no more. How could that possibly be? She was supposed to see me through life. What about all those great grandchildren I promised her? Were they going to grow up having never met one of the strongest influences in my life?

Added to that, I now felt that God had abandoned me. I was in a deep state of denial. None of this could possibly be real. My God would not desert me this way. I was going to wake up and laugh to myself for actually believing that any of this could be real. I mean, my life wasn't the greatest before, but this was going too far.

I began to doubt that there would ever be an end to this. I was destined to be unhappy for the rest of my life.

Grams

It came as a shock, we couldn't believe;
Nothing could prepare us for this.
Why did HE have to take you away?
Oh GRAMS, you'll truly be missed.

Your beautiful smile, your warm gentle touch,
All part of what made you YOU.
How could I go on not seeing your face?
God knows, I haven't a clue.

The lives that you touched, the love that you gave,
In our hearts those memories remain.
You've given so much and now that you're gone,
Life could never be the same.

With us for a time, that was His intent,
To give us your love and your care.
A blessing from heaven, ours just for a while,
Until your place, He could prepare.

God felt it was time to call you back home,
To take your place by His side.
And though we weren't ready, to let you go,
By His will we had to abide.

For you see, He has bigger plans for you,
You've completed your task here on earth.
It's time for you now, to take your true place,
Which He's marked for you from birth.

So now our precious angel has gotten her wings,
And is soaring high above.
Looking down on us with that special smile of hers,
And showering us with her love

So long, sweet GRAMS, spread your wings and fly,
For we know you'll always be near.
And with you up in heaven looking down on us,
I'm sure we'll have nothing to fear.

When?

The darkness consumes me.
I'm gasping for air.
Hands flailing wildly.
Is anyone there?

A cold hard vice,
Grabs hold of my heart.
It's squeezing and squeezing.
It's like I'm being torn apart.

My mind is deceiving me,
This cannot be real,
I'm going insane,
Can't describe how I feel.

My lungs fill with air now,
And I think I'm alright.
But it's trapped here inside me,
And my chest feels so tight.

Wake me up someone!
'cause this must all be a dream.
This madness is destroying me,
I just want to scream!

When will it all end?
When will I feel whole?
When will I smile again?
When will joy fill my soul?

Is Any of This Real?

Happiness…was it meant for everyone?
Is it something that really exists?
Or is it just a fantasy,
That we strive for, but always just miss?

Love…what does that even mean?
Some insist it's out there somewhere.
Or do we spend the rest of our lives,
Searching for something that's not even there?

Peace…we all talk about it,
But does anyone know what it is?
Can you ever find inner peace,
When in a world of turmoil you live?

Hope…now here's a good one,
An overused word, I would say.
It's so hard to be constantly hopeful,
When you face disappointment each day.

Faith…where do I even start?
What a cruel joke this must be!
Because I've had faith in so many people,
And look at where it's left me?

Joy…they say it comes from within,
But what if your life's filled with regret?
Where do you find this great joy,
On which you had your heart set?

Pain…now here's something real,
With which I'm sure we could all relate.
Because in life at some time or the other,
We've all had a full plate.

Sadness…it's all around us.
Everywhere you turn you can see,
Someone struggling with life,
Just trying to be happy.

Rejection…oh don't get me started,
Because to this there'll be no end.
For all through life we face it,
Hoping that our heart will mend.

Failure…an all too familiar truth,
Of which we've each had our share.
They say that quitters never win,
But sometimes your losses you just have to bear.

Depression…that's what it all comes down to,
This fact we just can't deny.
Each day we fight to make ourselves happy,
But what's the use, why even bother to try?

If my time here is one big test,
Then I can't shake the feeling I'm failing.
Where's the module I was meant to study?
Because without it, my whole life is derailing.

Is there any way to clean up this mess?
Does it make sense to even try?
Or do we go through this life pretending,
Until one day we all just die?

Living for Me

I take a deep breath and open the door.
For the world outside awaits.
I put on my smile, as I head on my way,
Because a whiner, everyone hates.

Good morning to all and have a nice day.
I make my way off to work.
Can't buckle now, everyone's watching,
But deep down inside, darkness lurks.

A nod of the head; a hearty hello,
To everyone that goes by.
Must put on a show; perform for them all,
When really, I just want to cry.

Get on with my work, keep myself occupied,
Find things to do all day long.
Everyone needs me to be super happy,
But in my heart, there's a melancholy song.

Friends pop in; they need my help.
For them, I'll never be busy.
I'll do anything; I'll always be there.
But when I call, it's not always that easy.

I think it's time I end this façade,
And start living my life for me.
Forget what they think; take time to heal.
From my monsters, I need to be free.

ANGER

At times it scares me the amount of anger I carried around inside. Anger towards family members, friends and the world in general. We have expectations of what relationships should be like. This isn't always the reality. For me, I had to learn the hard way that not everyone will be there for you when you need them. Maybe they can't. But for me, as I was going through my personal turmoil, I could only see the abandonment; the lack of care.

In our minds, parents are supposed to be there for us, no matter what. We expect them to be our rock; our source of strength. What we often forget, is that they too, have lives to deal with and can sometimes become overwhelmed by their own troubles. It is easy to become so consumed by one's anger and expectations that we selfishly blame others for our pain. For a long time I was blinded by the amount of anger I was holding on to and as a result, held several individuals responsible for my unhappiness.

I felt used and abused by so many. How could I ever possibly trust again? How could I let anyone in, when the ones who were supposed to be there for me turned their backs when I needed them most?

Ruined

So much of my life you've stolen from me,
While I just sat there and let it be.
I never fought back; I never complained.
I must admit, you had me well trained.

I lost who I was, while trying to please you.
To make you happy, there was nothing I wouldn't do.
I was a stranger to myself, my progress had been stunted.
And of that you took advantage, 'cause I was right where you wanted.

I no longer knew, what would make me truly happy.
It was all about you, and you liked that, didn't you hunny?
It was almost as if I could read your mind,
And before you even uttered a word, a solution I would find.

Don't even bother, to think about having friends.
For they all seemed a threat, so to that, I'd put an end.
You controlled and manipulated me, from the very start.
And as a preservation mechanism, I hardened my heart.

Everyone told me I needed to look out for you,
But what about me, didn't I need someone too?
I was only a child, yet I had to act older,
So I could carry the weight of you troubles on my shoulder.

So many times, I had the opportunity to grow.
Yet, you held on to me and wouldn't let go.
Obsessed and possessive, that's just what you were.
And so, the emotional abuse, I had to incur.

You stifled and smothered me, till I was nothing but a shell.
And the sad thing was, no one could tell.
I was good at pretending everything was alright,
And to see us together, was a beautiful sight.

I played along with your game, until I became a pro.
And all the suffering I dealt with, no one will ever know.
I couldn't have them, looking down on you.
So I took and I took, while inside I'd stew.

There were so many things, I wanted to do with my life.
I had dreams of one day being, a mother and a wife.
But just the thought that I'd be anything like you, was all it took,
To make me reconsider; take a second and third look.

And now, even after all of these years have gone by,
Why does the thought of you still make me cry?
I want to forgive you, God knows that's the truth.
But each time I come close, I'm transported to my youth.

I continue to lift you up, each time I pray,
And I hope I can let go of the hurt one day.
I no longer want to hold on to all this hate,
I want to forgive you, before it's too late.

God grant me the strength, to do what I know is right.
Help me to let go; to give up this fight.
I don't want to be bitter, I just want to heal.
And maybe one day, I'll know how true happiness feels.

Tired

Why is it so hard to understand,
That I too need time to heal?
Must I always be there for everyone,
And never spare a moment for me?

You judge me based on your beliefs,
Of what I ought to do.
Not once thinking to ask the question,
"My dear, and how are you"?

I'm tired of just succumbing,
To everyone's demands.
Why can't people just realize,
That I have my own life plans?

You forever have an opinion,
On how my life should be lived.
What I want doesn't really matter,
Once your input, you can give.

Do I ever try to control you?
Do I interfere in your life?
Have I ever been one to get involved,
To the point where I bring you strife?

I'll no longer be anyone's puppet.
My strings you will no more pull.
I'm living my life as I want to.
And you can bet it's going to be full.

You Promised

You promised you'd be there for me,
Through all my ups and downs.
You said you'd never leave my side,
Then things got turned around.

I trusted you to be my friend,
And share my hopes and dreams.
But now I see you've turned your back,
On all of that….. it seems.

What happened to the plans we had,
To make a difference together?
Was it not you who promised that,
We'd be best friends forever?

Were all those things you said to me,
All part of your charade?
I'm sorry, friend, to tell you that,
You didn't make the grade.

Too bad it took me all this time,
To finally realize,
That the person that I thought you were,
Was all a big disguise.

At least I know I'm strong enough,
To make it on my own.
For in spite of all the pain you've caused,
I know that I have grown.

So today *I* make a promise, that
This hurt will cease to be.
For I no longer wish to have,
All that you promised me.

No More

No more hurt, no more pain;
I just won't let you use me again.
I've been there for you, through the good and the bad,
And now that I need you, you think it's too hard.

I've stuck it out, when times were tough;
Don't you think, I've given enough?
I'm not going to be your stand-in girl.
I deserve someone who can give me the world.

For all those times, I've stood by you,
Can't you do the same for me too?
You've never had to ask me twice,
A little reciprocation would be nice.

I want to be the star of the show.
Is that too much to ask for, though?
I want to know I'm not taken for granted,
And what I do is appreciated.

So maybe it wasn't meant to be;
Me for you and you for me.
But I'll never forget the good times we had,
Thinking back now, it wasn't all bad.

And as we go our separate ways,
I'll always remember the happier days.
When things between us weren't so strained,
And the thought of you didn't cause me such pain.

I'll think of all the good times that we had.
Hold on to those memories, that don't make me sad.
Maybe one day, all this madness will end,
And we could go back to just being friends.

Wreckage

To be forgotten....
Cast aside like a piece of wreckage,
That has been washed ashore on a lonely beach,
Only to be pulled back in with the tide
And be lost at sea once more.
An existence so insignificant,
That it will never be remembered.
But alas, if it must be so,
Then such a fate must be accepted.
Battered by the waves,
As the tides come out once again.
Is it possible that it would be spotted this time,
And some use for it be imagined?
But regrettably, it's not to be,
As the surf's already determined its destiny.
And out into the vast sea it goes,
Floating aimlessly and unknown.

Free Me

Oh, how much I want to be whole again.
But no matter what I do, I just can't be,
For there are these fiends all around,
And they just won't set me free.

I find myself struggling day after day,
To break free of all these chains
That keep me captive and bound down,
But I cannot break my restraints.

I pull to the left and then to the right,
But the more I tug the worse it gets.
For you see, they've devised a fool-proof plan,
And I'm theirs until my death.

How I ended up in such a place,
I'll never comprehend.
Maybe they've taken me so long ago,
That I never even realized when.

I want to walk amongst the flowers
And see the sun as it rises in the morn.
But they've buried me so far away,
That I can't tell whether it's dusk or dawn.

What must I do to free myself?
I don't want to feel like this anymore.
I want to enjoy life to the fullest,
And not be trapped behind some door.

I want to see the world as others do,
To be happy and experience true love.
I want to laugh from way deep down inside,
And feel joy shining down from above.

Would any of this ever be possible for me?
I'm begging, Lord please say yes.
For you have certainly made me stronger,
If this was all a test.

I lay out my life to you, Dear Lord.
Take me and make me whole.
Wash away all of my sins, Father.
Cleanse my mind, body and soul.

Changing The Game

Don't play with my emotions,
Don't toy with my fragile heart.
I don't have time for these childish games,
I've told you that from the start.

Am I just fulfilling some fantasy,
That for a long time you've had?
Do I make you feel all alive again?
Did I save you from things that were bad?

Am I just some longtime desire,
That you needed to satisfy?
Do I bring out that special side of you,
When others never seemed to try?

What's this we're really doing?
Does it have any meaning for you?
Or is this just some game you're playing,
About which I haven't a clue?

I'd rather be alone and happy,
Than allow you a place in my life,
To open me up like some lab rat,
And rip out my heart with a knife.

So, make up your mind, my dear friend.
What is it you really want?
Am I just your little play thing?
Your flavor of the month?

The time has come for me to speak out.
I'm changing the rules of the game.
So, decide my dear, if you're up to it,
Because worse than this, I overcame.

BARGAINING

The bargaining stage for me, was quite short. I'm not sure if it is that I thought that I had nothing worth bargaining with, or the fact that I didn't feel that I needed much. I just wanted to be happy and whole; whatever that meant. Was that too much to ask for? I tried my best to live a good life and still, I was faced with all this negativity. I think I was too tired to bargain. I had lost all hope that things would ever get better, so what was the use in trying to make deals at this point? I was ready to give up.

Desires

I've never wanted anything this much.
I mean, there are things that I've once yearned for.
But this feeling I have, that something's missing,
Is rattling me to the core.

There's this void in my life, I can feel it.
And each day these emotions get stronger.
And I can't continue to fool myself;
I can't hide from these feelings much longer.

As children, we dream about our future,
And make all these elaborate plans.
But then life happens, and we realize,
That these decisions are not man's.

But that doesn't mean that the feelings,
Just suddenly slip away.
In fact, it's quite the opposite,
They get stronger and stronger each day.

Why can't I have this one desire fulfilled,
That will make me feel complete?
Don't I deserve a break in life?
Or has my disappointment been set on repeat?

I've made mistakes in my life, that's true.
But haven't we all done the same?
So why do I feel like I'm being punished,
Like I'm losing at life's difficult game?

Will I ever experience that happiness,
That so many others enjoy?
Or am I destined to live out my life,
Deprived of my share of joy?

No!.....*I* refuse to accept,
That I am not worthy of the best.
I'll continue to have faith,
And one day, with my dream, I'll be blessed.

Let's Make A Deal

Just this once, can't I be happy?
That's all I'm asking for.
I don't need a truckload of money.
Love's all I want, and I won't ask for more.

Give me this one thing and I'll be satisfied.
No need for anything else.
Someone who'll be there by my side,
While the world is wrapped up in itself.

Why can't I be one of the happy ones?
What's blocking me from this?
I've done my good deeds by the tons,
So why am I deprived of such bliss?

What do I really need to do?
Because right now, I'm not sure.
Why can't I have happiness too?
It's like something I can't afford in a store.

I see it; it's within my reach,
Then something gets in my way.
Like being at the market, reaching for that last peach,
And someone snatches it away.

Am I just one of the lonely few,
Who never finds true love?
Do I live out my life just dreaming of "You",
Hoping God is listening up above?

Can I just have this one little thing?
And for nothing more will I ask.
I just need something to make life worth living;
It doesn't seem such a big task.

Hold On Pain Ends

I can see in your eyes,
No point in trying to hide again.
Your tear-streaked face never lies,
You've been through so much pain.

You've been through so much pain,
That now it seems to be the norm.
And salty tears can't be washed away,
Not even the strongest of storms.

Not even the strongest of storms,
Can blow your hurt away.
This pain has taken on so many forms,
From your path, you fear you've strayed.

From your path you fear you've strayed,
And there's no way of coming back.
Everyone out there, has something to say,
But you alone are aware of the facts.

You alone are aware of the fact,
That your life has been derailed.
And confidence was never something you lacked,
Now you're beginning to feel like you've failed.

Now you're beginning to feel like you've failed;
Help doesn't seem to be coming from anywhere.
For so many nights, in bed, you've wailed.
Your only hope now is a prayer.

Your only hope now is a prayer.
So, you get on your knees and cry.
You know with God there's nothing to fear,
Now you're determined to give life a try.

Help

I'm tired Lord, this seems too much.
I've tried to be strong,
Even if it's just for your sake,
But something within me must be wrong

Why can't I just be happy?
It seems so easy for others.
What's it about me that's holding me back,
From forgetting my troubles and bothers?

I want to be a happy person,
But this seems to be eluding me.
How can I put aside all my woes,
And just let happiness be?

I know my mood sometimes affect,
The ones who really care.
But I don't know if they understand,
That there's little I can do, although I'm aware.

So many friends and supporters I'll lose,
If I continue along this path.
Lord this is something I want to fix,
And I mean it from the bottom of my heart.

Just give me the strength to make a start,
And from there, I'll give it a try.
I want to be happy like everyone else.
I no longer want to cry.

A Little Happiness

Just a little happiness,
Is all I ask for.
This one thing Lord,
And from you, I'll ask no more.

Help me smile and be carefree,
Give me strength to do your work.
I cannot get through this without you.
There's always that great sadness that lurks.

I want to be happy,
Don't think that I do not.
But it's always just out of my reach,
No matter what.

I need your help Lord,
To get through this time.
This is all I ask of you,
And after that, I'll be fine.

Not Today Satan

I've decided that I'm going to change my life,
But the devil just won't make it easy.
Each time I think I've gotten it right,
He comes up with a plan, oh so sleazy.

I fill my head with positive thoughts,
And he manages to get in between.
So, I'm battling to rid my mind of him,
But it's not as easy as it seems.

I wake up determined to have a good day,
But the snake from the Garden of Eden,
Has other plans and he just won't give up.
He thinks that he has me beaten.

Not today Satan, I repeat to myself,
As I go through my day bit by bit.
All of my trials, I put in the hand of the Lord,
And I know He can handle it.

DEPRESSION

As I mentioned earlier on, some stages lasted longer than others, and even seemed to come back just when I thought I was over with it.

I battled with depression for a long time and still do. In spite of what many people may think, it's not something that you can just "get over". And let us not confuse depression with sadness. We all feel sad at times for various reasons, but usually with the passing of time and some TLC, we can get through it and move on with our everyday lives.

Depression on the other hand is not quite as simple. According to the American Psychiatric Association, depression is referred to as a "common and serious medical illness that negatively affects how you feel, the way you think and how you act". It goes on to state that depression "causes feelings of sadness and loss of interest in activities once enjoyed. It can lead to emotional and physical problems and decrease a person's ability to function at work and at home".

For me, one of the most difficult parts of dealing with depression was the feeling that I needed to do it on my own. I couldn't let anyone know how I was feeling. That would be a sign of weakness, and that was one thing I never wanted to be thought of as. So I kept it all inside. At work, I would smile with everyone. I maintained a very professional front, giving the impression that I was living the perfect life. Little did they know that I cried myself to sleep at night, just praying for the morning to come quickly so that I didn't have to spend so much time with my own thoughts.

It was much easier with family members. You see, I was never one to socialize much, so when I missed a family function or any other celebration, it didn't come as a surprise. No one expected me to show up anyway. Chances are, many didn't even notice that I was not present.

Not to make this all about depression, but for me this was the most difficult stage. It lasted the longest and at times when I felt like it might be over, it reared its ugly head again. These were some of the darkest times in my life; times that I felt so alone. One of the things that kept me sane in these times was my writing. I was able to truly express my feelings without actually letting anyone in.

Don't be confused, during this stage it was not all dark skies. I often hoped that things could be better. The problem was, I didn't know how to make it better. Sitting around and waiting for something to happen was exhausting. During these times I always felt that I would be ready if God called me home.

The very first poem in this set, was written when I was just nine years old. Looking back now, I feel sad for that little girl who had to feel this way. She, like me, kept it all inside and tried to handle it all by herself. Maybe, just maybe, if she had gotten the help then.........................

Did You Ever...

Did you ever feel so sad,
So sad that you cannot say,
And did you ever wish
That someone would come your way?

Did you ever feel afraid?
Afraid of what you cannot say?
Did you ever wish, that you had a friend,
With whom you can play?

Did you ever feel so lonely,
As though you were all alone?
And did you ever wish?
That you had someone to hug you,
Someone who will always be there for you?
Did you ever?

Who Am I

I've lost who I am,
Not sure who I should be.
For so long I've pretended,
Now I don't know the real me.

Growing up as a child,
I followed the lead
Of those all around me,
Succumbing to their needs.

I've tried so very hard,
To please everyone.
Giving all of myself,
Even when for me it was no fun.

I've been living a lie
All these years,
Thinking that I was strong,
Now, I can't stop the tears.

A picture of confidence,
I portrayed for the world.
My masks were convincing,
A performance, worthy of gold.

I had them all fooled.
They never could tell,
That deep down inside,
I was living in hell.

It's getting much harder now,
To keep up the charade.
But I can't let them see,
Of what I'm really made.

So, I try a little more.
A greater effort I make,
To keep that smile on my face,
Even though it may be fake.

Disappointments

Perhaps some things just aren't meant to be.
Not all dreams become reality.
Even when human eyes fail to see,
We must accept it, though painfully.

Not because you want it so,
Means that these ideas of yours will grow.
Sometimes, you just need to let go,
And maybe the reason, someday, you'll know.

Disappointments, we face them every day.
Seemingly blue skies just turn to grey.
And when all hope is washed away,
All there's left to do is pray.

You hope that someday you'll get over it,
Those strong desires you once had, would quit.
But then at night, by yourself, you sit,
And the truth of it suddenly seems to hit.

How could you have been such a fool?
You've never been one to follow the rule.
And lying in bed those tears just pool,
Thinking about how life can be so cruel.

What could you have done to deserve all this pain?
Sometimes you feel like you're going insane.
All life within you, just seems to drain.
And any hope for happiness, is now all in vain.

When it comes to love, you've never been much of a fan.
So, why's it so hard for you to understand?
Did you think you could just wave some magic wand,
And your negativity would wash away with the waves, like sand?

Maybe one day from these desires you'll be free,
And go on living life happily.
But until then, you'll have to accept and agree,
That perhaps, some things just aren't meant to be.

My Demons

I'm stifling, I'm struggling, and I cannot breathe.
It feels like a plastic bag's been placed over my head.
And the fear inside me begins to seethe;
Someone or something wants me dead.
I pull this way and that, but it's all in vain.
For the more that I fight it, the worse things get.
Now I cannot think; I'm in so much pain.
It's like I'm paying off some unknown debt.
I try to scream out, but no sound escapes.
Not that it matters, 'cause no one seems to care.
In the distance, I think I see some human-like shapes.
But when I look again, there's nobody there.
"What's happening to me?" my mind wants to shout,
As I pull and tug at my tightening restraints.
And just when I think, I might find a way out,
Lightheaded, I take a deep breath, then I faint.........

I open my eyes and can't believe what I see;
I'm in this bright room all alone.
A peaceful silence surrounds me,
And I feel like, strangely, I've grown.
The funny thing is, this time I don't feel lonely.
The quiet seems to be just what I need.
Dare I say, it even feels a bit Holy?
For now, I feel like I've been freed.
Embraced by the light that now flows in,
A bright smile adorns my face.
For the big ugly demon, I'd been battling,
Cannot enter my happy place.
I take a deep breath and spread my arms wide,
As I look to the bright morning sun.
Never again will I need to hide,
For this battle of mine, I've won.

Alone

I open my eyes,
And all I see is darkness.
I'm standing in the middle of nowhere,
The world no longer exists.

I look to left and right…..
But nothing catches my eye.
Panic begins to take over,
And all I can do is cry.

Where has everyone gone?
And why am I still here?
This must be some kind of joke.
The quiet, I can no longer bear.

I'm trying to scream,
But no sound comes out.
What's going on here?
Why can't I open my mouth?

This loneliness is killing me.
Can't take this anymore.
Is there some purpose for this suffering?
What am I here for?

I just want to see another face,
Hear another voice,
But I'm stuck here in this void,
And I don't have a choice.

Why is this happening to me?
What have I done?
Why can't I be free?
When will this feeling be gone?

And suddenly, out of nowhere,
A bright light appears.
And just as unexpectedly,
I'm surrounded by my peers.

But they still seem so far away,
And it's then, I realize how it's meant to be.
That no matter who's there,
It'll always be, "just me"…..

The Hole

For most of my life, I lived in a hole.
And I was nothing but content.
For I made myself believe that,
That's what happiness meant.

I went along my way each day,
With not the slightest care.
Never once thinking that just maybe,
There was something more out there.

But then one day, things changed.
And I wasn't sure what it could be.
Did I get too big for the hole?
Or did it get too small for me?

For suddenly, I felt stifled.
I could stay in there no more.
I pushed and pushed against the walls,
Trying to find the door.

I couldn't breathe, I panicked.
I needed to get out.
I yelled at the top of my lungs,
But no one could hear my shouts.

It was then, that I decided,
That this was something I must do.
I clawed and clawed until,
I could see light shining through.

Little by little I chip away,
At this hole I let devour me.
And though I have a long way to go,
I know, one day I'll be free.

Help Me

I lie awake and just let the tears flow,
Down my cheek and I don't even know
Why I continue to feel the way,
That I do each and every day.

Perhaps somewhere along the path I strayed,
And now I can't seem to find my way
Back to the place I ought to be,
Where God had once intended for me.

Or maybe this is some big trick,
That's being played on me, but it seems so sick
To have me feel like such a waste,
That simply takes up unnecessary space.

Oh, how I wish I knew the source,
Of all this pain, but then of course
What would I do if I discover,
That from this hurt I'll not recover?

Should I then accept the hand,
That life has dealt me, is this my plan
To go on living day by day,
Being pulled each and every way?

Sometimes I just want to put an end to it,
And leave this world in which I don't seem to fit.
Or just as well disappear,
To a place where I have no more fear.

What use am I to anyone,
All damaged and broken, my life undone?
How can I help someone out there,
When for myself I can't even care?

Oh Lord, I pray you'd help me to,
Figure out what I must do.
'cause as it is, I'm really lost,
And I'm scared that it's my life, it will cost.

Drowning

Waves crashing…..
The current pulling me in.
I'm drowning, someone help me!
I don't know how to swim.

I struggle to the surface,
But it's all in vain.
Because with another big crash,
I'm under, once again.

Reaching out for something,
Anything, to grab hold of.
But only sand slips through my fingers,
As I look to the sky above.

A lull in the madness,
And I can now see the shore.
I'm waving and shouting,
Till I can't breathe anymore.

And just when I think,
That it's coming to an end,
A huge wave grabs me from behind,
Like a long, lost friend.

I'm pulled back in,
And it all seems too late.
With the shore no longer in sight,
I accept my fate…..

I allow my weightless body,
To be pulled to the sea floor.
The struggling now stops,
I can't fight it anymore.

Looking up at the sky,
Through the clear blue sea,
I think about my life,
And how it came to be.

What Happened?

I really thought things had finally changed.
I was having such a good day.
The masks I wore for all these years,
Were slowly, peeling away.

I woke in the morning, all ready to go,
To take on everything out there.
I walked out and about with such confidence,
For I knew I had nothing to fear.

The sun seemed much brighter, the air so fresh.
I was seeing things I'd never seen before.
So much of the world, I'd been missing out on,
And to think there was so much more.

…But then it happened, like I was sure it would,
For I knew it was never meant to be.
What on earth would make me think,
That happiness was intended for me?

Suddenly, the sky didn't seem so bright.
And the air, had a rancid smell.
Once again, I was holding back tears,
That alone in my room, just fell.

What happened to make it turn all around?
I wanted so much for it to be true.
Now, all I have are these negative thoughts,
And I don't know what to do.

God, help me, I pray, for I really don't know,
How much more of this I can take.
It takes so much out of me to walk around,
With a smile that's nothing but fake.

I want to see a blue sky and be filled with joy,
Have the sunshine just light up my day.
Feel laughter bubbling up from my soul,
For this, oh Lord, I pray.

Burdens

This heaviness I carry around inside of me,
I'm just not sure how I really feel.
Why can't I understand this pain,
That seems to be driving me insane?

Thoughts swirling around inside my head,
Sometimes, I feel I'd be better off dead.
I can't control my emotions anymore.
It's almost like an internal war.

God, please just take this cup away,
I can no longer cope; for peace I pray.
Why, oh Lord, must I always feel like this?
I've prayed…I've cried…I've begged…I've wished.

SOMEONE! ANYONE! Hear my cry.
I don't want to live, I'd rather just die.
This burden is too much to bear.
Is anyone out there? Can anyone hear?

I want to be happy; I want to be free.
So why do these demons keep haunting me?
My life wasn't supposed to be this way.
Lord, tell me what happened; where did I stray?

Pretending is so much harder these days.
I walk around with a fake smile on my face.
But how much longer can I keep this up?
I just want these bad feelings to stop.

I wait for the day when my smile will be real,
And I have no problem saying how I feel.
But for now, I'll just bury it all inside,
And keep strutting around like someone, filled with pride.

Just Let Me Be

They can't understand it,
Even if they try.
The times when it gets bad,
I'd rather just die.

They think that they're helping,
But just make things worse.
Why can't they just leave me?
My life feels so cursed.

I don't need your assistance!
I'm good on my own.
I'm used to just handling,
My issues alone.

Please try to understand,
I'm not being rude.
But the more that you push,
The more stress I exude.

I just want to be happy.
But that's up to me.
You can't take my burdens;
So just let me be.

Do you really care,
Or is this just about you?
Can I trust that you're genuine,
In the things that you do?

I want to be able,
To accept your help.
But right now, I just need
To do this myself.

Maybe one day, I can help you
To understand how I feel.
But for now, you'll just have to
Let me take the wheel.

Loneliness

Is anyone there?
Someone.......Anyone......Can you hear me?
I'm so scared,
I feel so alone,
It's so quiet, so dark,
I'm cold,
Can anyone hear me?
I'm so afraid,
My heart beats faster, it's pounding,
I can't breathe,
Where is everyone?
Wait....I see them, but they are so far away
Someone! Help me, please!
No one hears my cries,
They don't see me, they can't hear me.
They are all around me, yet I feel so alone.
I need help....Please....Anyone?
I can't take it, I can't......
Wait! A whisper...."Don't give up!"
........Someone's there.
I hear Him calling.
Oh no.....I'm so afraid!
'Fear Not My Child, For I Am Here'
That voice! So soft.
Those words! So soothing, so Comforting.
Suddenly, I'm no longer afraid.
Someone's there, I can feel His presence.
I know He's real.
He speaks to me.
I feel safe....I AM Safe.
He'll protect me.
He'll always be there.

I'll never be alone.
I never have to worry again.
I don't have to do it alone.
HE'S HERE WITH ME, HE'LL HELP ME.

Sinking

I'm sinking deeper and deeper,
And no one can see
The pain and the heartache,
That lives within me.

They look at my smile,
And think all is well.
When really, I just feel
Like I'm living in hell.

This dark cloud of depression,
Consumes my every thought.
And there's just no more energy,
For so long I've fought.

They just don't understand!
"Be positive," they say.
But if it was that easy,
Would I allow myself to feel this way?

I just want it to end,
One way or the other.
This feeling of hopelessness,
I can't take any longer.

Lord Father I pray,
That you'll give me the strength,
To face each new day,
And go the full length.

I don't want to be weak,
But I can fight no more.
I need You Dear Father.
Help me feel secure.

I Never

I've never been in love before.
That's what I once believed.
But true love takes on different forms,
Far from what I had conceived.

I've never had a broken heart.
That's what I used to say.
Until the day that heart ache,
Came crashing down my way.

I never knew I could feel like this,
As if my world would end.
Now I can't help but thinking,
That I just lost a friend.

I never ever expected,
To feel such pain inside.
But now each day I wake up,
Like piece of me has died.

I never thought that I would
Allow myself to grieve,
So much for one who clearly,
Didn't cherish me.

I never thought that I would be,
One of the weaker ones,
Who cries herself to sleep at night,
And at morning, a smile dons.

So, now I know what it feels like,
To be this torn apart.
I never will allow another,
To wreak havoc with my heart.

I've Been Missing Out

I never knew what I was missing out on,
Until the scales were removed from my eyes.
Now I'm finding it hard to go on,
Knowing that I was just living a lie.

I thought I was happy, but none of it was real.
I made myself believe I was content.
But now I'm beginning to know how it feels
To be lonely; and this feeling, I resent.

There's an emptiness deep down inside of me,
That I'm unable to fill on my own.
And I can't shake this feeling, that I should be
Trying to find my way home.

How could I have been so blind all these years?
Not knowing that I could have more.
Was it because I had all of these fears,
Of being hurt right down to the core?

Why must I succumb to all these emotions,
That break my heart more each day?
Maybe the numbness was a better notion,
At least I didn't hurt that way.

I want to experience true love at its best,
To be treated the way I deserve.
Not lumped in there, with all the rest,
On the bench, like some kind of reserve.

Perhaps someday, I'll find the one out there,
Who would give to me all of the world.
But for now, I'll just have to make myself happy.
Love myself, for all that I'm worth.

The End

It's done…too late to turn back now.
She's made her decision,
And stuck to her vow….
She can only hope it's as she envisioned.

She lies there peacefully;
Life slipping away,
And all she remembers,
Are the happier days.

Her mum, there beside her,
Cheering her on.
In mummy's eyes,
She could do no wrong.

And loved ones smiling on,
Around her, arms curled.
Reminding her daily,
That she could take on the world.

A peacefulness comes over her,
And a smile crosses her face.
She's finally leaving,
This stifling place.

A knock on the door…
But it's already too late.
She thinks for a moment,
And in her heart, there's no hate.

She closes her eyes,
And whispers a prayer,
For her family and friends
All those she holds dear.

She prays He'll forgive her,
For what she has done.
But, He knew all her struggles,
Each and every one.

The time finally comes,
And she takes one last breath…
Hoping the happiness, she didn't find in life,
She'll finally, find in death…

Life

Have you ever had the feeling
That your life had passed you by,
And still so much you had to do,
But not quite enough time?

At night, I lie awake in bed,
With sleep so far away.
I think about my troubled life,
And how it got this way.

I've tried to be more positive,
And not let doubt creep in.
But then that inner turmoil starts,
And crazy thoughts begin.

I had so many childhood dreams,
Of how my life would be.
But they all seem so far off now,
A distant memory.

A doctor or a lawyer, sure,
That's what I want to be.
I'll probably save the world one day,
And make them all happy.

I watched my youth just slip away,
Gone without a trace.
And all I have are regrets now,
That seem to take its place.

Was this God's master plan for me,
That I should die like this?
With nothing to be remembered for,
Not sure that I'll be missed.

Alone and in a dark place now,
I think the time draws near,
When I must leave my earthly home
And go far away from here.

But wait, I see a shining light.
There's someone here with me.
He's reaching out, to take my hand,
And suddenly I feel free.

"My child," He says, "Don't look so sad.
Your life was not in vain,
You have fulfilled my plans for you,
Faithful, you have remained."

"You've always been a source of strength,
For those who've lost their way,
Thinking that life was not worthwhile,
And thus, begin to stray."

"You've opened up your heart and mind,
To allow God's love inside,
And shared this love with those around,
Brining joy to those who cried."

"So now, my child, it's time to go,
To your Father up above.
But your memory will still live on,
In those you gave your love."

ACCEPTANCE

For me the word "acceptance" held several different meanings. I accepted that this was *my* life and if I wanted to see a change, I had to be willing to make that change. I accepted that in life, things don't always play out the way you want them to. Sometimes you just have to "roll with the punches". I accepted that, although there were those who contributed to my current situation, I had to find it in myself to forgive and let go. I accepted that this is something that I will have to live with for the rest of my life, but *I* will determine how I'm affected by it. I've accepted that not everyone will understand, and that's alright. I've accepted that sometimes it's necessary to let others in, for the real healing to take place. I've accepted that it's alright to open up myself to receive love. I have accepted that I am worthy of goodness and happiness, and there's beauty out there within my reach. All I need to do is reach out and grab hold of it.

This new-found acceptance has allowed me to be more appreciative of all that is around me. I can now step outside and admire the beauty of a sunrise or the dew drops on a leaf; things that I had shut myself off from in the past. I cherish the strong relationships I have built and freely let go of the ones that no longer exist.

Acceptance doesn't mean that I'm no longer afraid. Life is scary; living life with depression is terrifying. What this acceptance does is, allow me to claim good for myself. No longer will I think that I'm not worthy enough or deserving enough. With this acceptance, I'm allowing happiness to enter my life and I'm going to be the one controlling it.

Most importantly, I accept that on my journey to healing, there are those I may have hurt. For this I am genuinely sorry.

Sorry

It was never my intention to hurt you,
To put you in the middle of this.
You won't believe how much each day,
Our times together I miss.

I wish I could go back in time,
And change things, just for you.
But it's not that very easy.
You see, this is something I must do.

You've become an important part of my life,
This will forever be true.
And no matter where the wind may blow us,
Just know that I'll always love you.

I pray for you each morning,
Asking God to guide your way.
To keep you safe and close to Him,
As you go about your day.

I've watched you grow throughout the years,
Into a young lady, both beautiful and smart.
Always thinking about those around you,
And giving with a generous heart.

I know that you'll always excel,
At whatever you set your mind to.
So, just keep believing in yourself,
Like I believe in you.

Maybe one day things will go back,
To the way they used to be.
But for now, I want you to remember,
That you can forever, count on me.

Momma

I know you did all that you could,
To ensure that my life was good.
And though at times, it was kind of rough,
You just kept pushing so I'd have enough.

There were times I felt as though,
That more than me, you needed to grow.
But now I understand that it might have been tough,
Having to deal with your own stuff.

You tried so hard to hold it together,
You were everyone's rock in the stormiest of weather.
But there came a point you could be strong no more,
And you let your defenses just slip to the floor.

That was the time I needed you most,
But you couldn't be there, and I just felt so lost.
You're the one who's supposed to be strong.
Everything now feels so very wrong.

I tried so hard to hold you up,
But I resented the fact, that I had to carry this cup.
Aren't you supposed to look out for me?
This is not how things are supposed to be.

Everyone expected me to be there for you.
No one ever had a clue,
That I was suffering deep down inside,
And needed my momma to be by my side.

Don't mean to sound selfish, but that's how I feel.
These feelings I'm carrying around inside are real.
I just want to be able to hear you say,
"Don't worry my love, everything will be okay."

I love you mom, more than you will ever know,
Although at times it may not show.
I think about you all through the day,
And for your happiness and health, I always pray.

I know it wasn't always easy for you,
But you did all that you could do.
You've made me the woman I am today,
So, thank you momma, is all I can say

Reclaiming My Life

I'm putting an end to this nonsense.
I'm tired of all of these games.
It's gone on way too long,
And now, my life, I must reclaim.

There's a world of opportunities out there.
I'm finally opening my eyes to see,
That I am deserving of happiness.
There are good things in store for me.

My future now seems so much brighter.
And that weight I've been carrying, is gone.
And though at times it didn't feel right,
Sometimes, you just have to move on.

I'm letting go of all the pain,
That has kept me submissive for years.
I'm ready to take on new challenges,
There's no more time for tears.

The world out there awaits me,
And nothing will hold me back.
It's time I put to good use,
This courage that I once lacked.

So, look out world, I'm coming!
Prepare yourselves for a new me.
It's about time I start doing.
I'm done with just letting things be.

True Love

For the first time in my life,
I know how true love feels.
I've spent some time getting to know,
What's fake and what is real.

Those quiet days, spent all alone,
Gave me some time to think.
And now I know I had it wrong,
As I watch the bad memories sink.

See, I've been looking for love,
Searching both high and low.
Trying to find that someone out there,
The thought of whom, will make me glow.

But a deeper look inside myself,
While basking in this tranquil place.
Helped me to see that love exists,
If only I'd make the space.

Sitting and looking out at the vastness,
Of the never-ending sea,
I've come to realize the truth,
That true love lies inside of me.

For how can anyone claim,
To be in love with someone else?
When the truth is, you've never learnt,
To truly love yourself.

So today I make this promise,
That has finally set me free.
I'll forever cherish what's important.
For I've found my true love, and it's me...

Once I Was Lost

There once was a time I just wished I would die;
I couldn't make myself happy, no matter how hard I tried.
Nothing I did seemed to be going my way,
But through it all I continued to pray.

Those negative thoughts, I tried to push deep down inside;
No one could know what I was thinking, so these feelings I'd hide.
But soon I realized this wasn't working out for me,
And if I wanted to recover, I'd need to speak to somebody.

You'd be surprised, what opening up can do,
You discover things about yourself that you never even knew.
At times it was hard, but I kept plodding on,
Hoping that someday, these feelings would be gone.

True friends popped up, where I never expected.
And know it or not, my life they affected.
A side of me came out, that I never knew was there.
And of the depth of my worth, I'm now very clear.

Today I stand tall, with visions in sight.
Knowing that once I apply myself, with all my might,
That these visions will one day, become a reality.
Much thanks to all those, standing beside me.

When I Fall In Love

When I fall in love…..
……. That must be a joke!
Because from where I'm standing,
Love's not, for normal folks.

That made up stuff,
You see on the tv.
Where boy falls for girl,
And they're so, so happy.

They hug and they kiss,
Declaring undying love.
Then run off together,
Surrounded by doves.

None of that's real.
It's all just for show.
Real love is just heartache,
Then, someone must go.

Don't think that I'm bitter,
I'm just telling the truth.
Love's not for the weak-hearted.
Leave that for the youth.

I'd rather be alone,
With my heart still in tact.
Than venture into love,
And then regret the act.

So what if I spend my days,
All by myself....
At least my heart will be safe,
Somewhere high on a shelf.

.........But, is it so bad
To want to be with someone,
Who makes you feel,
You're their moon and their sun?

To be treated as if,
You're their everything.
And that with you,
Their life has new meaning.

So maybe I'll give
This whole love thing a go.
When I fall in love.....
......I'll let you know.

Hold Me

Hold me …..
Just put your arms around me and squeeze.
Tell me…..
That I am all that you'll ever need.
Hug me…..
Don't let go even for a while.
Love me…..
Promise you'll stay by my side.
Please me…..
Do all that you know I desire.
Caress me…..
Set my body and soul on fire.
Inspire me…..
To be all you know I can be.
Protect me…..
With you I want to be free.
Help me…..
Chase all my demons away.
Assure me…..
That by my side you will stay.
Kiss me…..
Till all of this pain is no more.
Touch me…..
Just please don't walk out the door.

Love Overload

Stripped of my defenses,
Standing vulnerable in your wake.
Before you, I feel so exposed,
And I don't know how much more I can take.

You've brought out certain sides of me,
That I never even knew existed.
And even when I tried to deny these feelings,
You never gave up, you persisted.

Where would I be if I hadn't met you?
What path would my life have taken?
So many wonders, I'd have missed out on,
All those dreams I'd have forsaken.

Where have you been all my life?
Why has it taken you so long to get here?
It's funny, but I think with you beside me,
I would never have shed a tear.

When you look at me the way you do,
My heart feels like it's about to explode.
I'm no longer in control of my emotions.
Is there such a thing as love overload?

Each time that we're together,
It's like I'm starting all over again.
Will I ever get used to this feeling,
That my life's no longer about pain?

You bring out the very best in me.
That's one thing I know for sure.
I only hope I can give back to you,
All you've given to me, and more.

Thank you for all these memories,
That I'll forever keep with me.
See, you've made me a brand-new person.
Or was it that, you just set me free?

The Beauty of Morning

Sitting alone as I watch the sun rise,
Sipping coffee from my favourite cup.
The stillness around me is such a surprise,
It's like the rest of the world's not yet up.

The cool morning air makes me feel so alive,
And I'm ready to take on the world.
Into this new day, I'm willing to dive,
The prospects are worth more than gold.

It's amazing the beauty you see all around,
While the rest of the world is asleep.
And in your mind, this day, for goodness you're bound,
Just be brave and take that big leap.

During these times, I can call on the Lord,
And ask Him to take control of my day.
For I know that without the strength from God,
Things certainly won't go my way.

Morning Glory

The beautiful morning, what an amazing sight!
Covered with the morning mist,
The sun peeping out from behind.
A sight that no one should miss.

The clear blue skies, as the morning begins.
Just breathe in that clean fresh air.
So often we busily go about our day,
And of these wonders, we are not aware.

Why would anyone want to spend the morning indoors?
When there's so much beauty outside.
So much of God's blessings we're missing out on,
When in our bedrooms we choose to hide.

The morning sun, when it finally shows its face,
Is such a sight to behold.
On your skin, it warms you up ever so slightly,
Getting rid of the lingering cold.

A hummingbird, stopping to drink at a flower.
That's something you don't see every day.
But sitting outside, as the sun begins to rise,
To these little blessings, homage I pay.

How truly blessed we all must be,
To be privy to all of this beauty.
So why not take the time out once in a while,
And appreciate the work of His Majesty?

Self Love

Although at times the world seems a dreadful place,
There's still so much beauty around.
Just close your eyes, and take a deep breath,
And listen to the awesome sounds.

Looking up at the sky, I feel the presence of God.
So much He has given to us.
The birds and the flowers and the trees so tall,
There's no doubt He loves us; He must.

Each life is precious, we must realize,
For these bodies of ours are on loan.
Be good to yourself and always remember,
To take care of this temple, you call home.

Love yourself for who you are.
No one out there can be a better you.
So, don't be distracted, by what others may have,
You just go on doing what you have to do.

At the end of the day, when you lay your head down,
You're the one who'll be called upon,
To answer for all of the choices you made,
And take responsibility, for all that you've done.

Family

If you think that family is all about blood,
Then my friend, you're very much mistaken.
Because friends who stick by you when you're down,
Are the ones who won't leave you forsaken.

"Friends turn Family", that's what I call them,
And know that you'll never be alone,
For they go out of their way to look after you,
Make you feel like one of their own.

I've been blessed throughout life, with people like this,
Who've gone out of their way to accept me.
So, no matter how bad things may get sometimes,
I know by my side they will be.

I thank God for them, each and every one,
Who's stood by me during my trials.
And His blessings I pray for them one and all,
May He walk with them all the while.

Friendship

True friendships are formed, when you least expect it.
Not everyone you meet,
Will be the right fit.

But when you're not looking, someone comes your way.
And to your amazement,
They'll know just the right things to say.

Sometimes we go out, thinking we will find,
The one who will be there,
For us at just the right time.

Quite often the decision, is not ours to make.
You'll go through so many,
Many of whom will be fake.

Be patient, and don't be too quick to rush in.
What seems good at first,
Might cause you great pain.

The one who's really for you, will be there.
Sometimes you just need to open your eyes,
And be a little more aware.

No one was meant, to handle this world alone.
So fear not, you just wait,
You'll find the right one.

Be Free

It's time to put all negativity aside,
And start living this life full of self-pride.
You don't need a handbook or any such guide,
Just let go, be free and enjoy the ride.

There's too much out there, that you can do nothing about,
So why's it when things don't go as planned you pout.
Maybe life is telling you, there's an alternative route,
One that will see that from this painful situation you get out.

Smile and be happy and good to those you can.
Whenever the opportunity offer a helping hand.
This world will be so much better, if together we band.
Look out for one another, each and every man.

I'm Ready

I'm ready to be happy now,
Just watch out world and see.
All the troubles I've been holding on to,
It's time for me to set them free.

I'm reaching out for goodness,
And I shall not be distracted.
I've done my time and now I believe,
I'm headed for things more constructive.

It's time for me to stop chasing my dreams,
And get serious and hold them down.
Too much of my life I spent regretting,
The things I should have done.

No more waiting for the future,
It's time to act right now.
Though obstacles may stand in my way,
I'll find a path somehow.

I'm done with making excuses,
The onus is on me,
To do the things that I must do,
To make myself happy.

REFLECTION

Having gone through (and still going through in some cases) these five stages, I can honestly say I have grown. I see life differently now. It's still not a perfect life, but I can recognize, not only the good in my life, but also all the ways that I can make a difference in the lives of others.

Believe me, the last thing someone who is afflicted wants to hear is, "You should be grateful, there are so many people out there who have it worse than you do". Despite the good intentions, it does nothing to help. You are now drawn deeper into yourself as you are made to feel that your pain and suffering are not important enough to be paid attention to.

But, going through what I've had to deal with, has made me more sensitive to the plight of others. There are people out there suffering, both young and old. Many of them have mastered the art of acting, as I did for so many years. It's funny how we can spend so much time with a person and not be aware of the pain they are carrying around inside.

Parents, it's important to pay close attention to your children. It's so easy to get caught up in your personal struggles and miss the little cues. What at first seems like an insignificant change, may be a cry for help. Let's not wait until it's too late and then say, "I should have known." These are our kids, let's take care of them and ensure that there's a future of strong, healthy and productive leaders.

This section is dedicated to those who suffer silently. It is up to us to look out for the signs and do all in our power to help those who are struggling. The signs are there, we just need to pay attention. You'd be surprised the difference you can make in someone's life by just being there for them.

Teenage Pegnancy

Innocence lost…no turning back.
Forced to be a grownup…
Struggling to keep her life on track.

Teenage years…expecting to be free.
But instead, life upside down…
Because now she's raising a baby.

The alternatives seemed, too hard to bear.
Abortion was suggested…
But the consequences she feared.

Heard of the girl, who gave hers away.
Couldn't deal with the stress…
Now thinks of her baby, night and day.

So how exactly did it come to this?
Rape and incest…
The signs clear but were all missed.

Absent father, what else is expected?
No true role model,
To teach her how she should be treated.

So, when one day, he came on the scene,
Who could blame her?
She was only just a teen.

He said all the things, she wanted to hear.
Made her feel wanted…
For once, someone cared.

Late that night, when he came into her room,
And put his cold hand on her...
With fear, she was consumed.

Shhh.... he told her, with finger on lips,
As he moved in closer...
Caressing her ample hips.

The experience was awful, she'd never forget.
But as he left, he reminded her,
This was their little secret...

Night after night, it was all the same.
But what could she do?
She was filled with such shame.

All through the day, she walked with head hanging down.
But no one ever noticed,
Just happy to have a strong man around.

Several times, she almost relented and told.
But the fear came over her,
And the details she decided to withhold.

Finally, the day came when she thought she would die.
Found out she was pregnant,
Now all she could do was cry.

Couldn't keep it a secret, from others much longer.
So, she got up the courage,
And finally, the words she did utter.

Never before, had she seen such rage.
"What are you going to do with a child,
At this very young age?"

She tried to explain that it wasn't her fault.
But nothing could protect her,
From the verbal assault.

"Stop telling lies on such a good guy,
He's been here for us always,
Now this is what you try!"

"You little whore, get out of my house!
Sneaking around behind my back,
While acting like a little mouse!"

So out on the streets, with no hope in sight,
Desperate and alone,
She doesn't have the strength to fight.

Family and friends want no part of her.
But determined she was,
To make things turn out better.

Now one year late, at the age of fifteen,
A mother and provider,
Not exactly her life's dream.

Many times, things seemed tough and she almost gave in.
But he'd ruined her life once before,
Now she refused to let him win.

At no time, would she claim that it wasn't a struggle.
But with all the right help,
Her situation, she now handles.

You Should Have Listened

She tried her best to hide the pain,
No one needed to know.
And though at times, it was a strain,
She struggled to put on a show.

At first it was just the things he said,
That made her feel unwanted.
But then, the marks on her skin, bright red,
Caused her every thought to be haunted.

Each time she heard the sound of his voice,
Her heart would skip a beat.
But she'd sit in wait, she hadn't a choice,
As she shuddered at approaching feet.

The reason each time, she never knew.
But the feeling was always the same.
The crack of the belt and the pain grew,
As he shouted angrily, her name.

The beatings were worse, after a night at the bar.
At these times, he didn't hold back.
So, she'd close her eyes and think of places so far,
As she winced with every whack.

Protector, what a joke, she was no use.
She just stood there during each beating.
Could it be, she lived through her share of abuse,
And was now happy she was no longer a victim?

To cope with the pain, she made herself numb.
And oversized sweatshirts each day she would wear.
For the questions that came, her answers were dumb,
These were things she just couldn't share.

Soon, it got to the point where she felt nothing at all.
The blows and the punches didn't matter.
In the shower, however, she'd let the tears fall,
As the cuts and bruises burned in the water.

This straight A student, was now struggling in school,
But no one took the time to ask why.
They should have known that she was no fool,
Instead, they all turned a blind eye.

One day, sitting alone in her room on the bed,
She found a razor nearby.
And for just a second, the thought entered her head,
"Maybe it would be better if I die."

Slowly, she brought it up to her skin,
And the feel of the metal was comforting.
If she did this, would it mean that he'd win?
Is this just what he'd been expecting?

The very first cut, as the blade made contact,
And the blood slowly ran down her arm.
She knew there and then, there was no turning back,
Her only escape was self-harm.

How had things taken such a turn?
She never got a real chance at life.
Now she lay on the bed, with cuts that burn,
As she let go of all of her strife.

She closes her eyes and the silence is broken,
As they both burst through her door.
With her last bit of breath, final words are spoken,
She doesn't have to hold back anymore.

"You, standing there, what are you crying for?
You knew what I was going through.
Didn't you think at the time, you could have done more?
Instead, you thought of how it would affect you."

"And you, my abuser; for it's the only fitting name,
For that's the only role you could play.
My only regret in this whole game,
Is that for your deeds, you never will pay.

A peaceful feeling comes over her,
As she feels life slipping away.
Maybe she never got to experience happiness on earth,
But she knew it would be hers today…

Voices In My Head

What is it these voices have against me?
Why can't they go away, so I can be happy?
But of course, it all seems so lonely,
When they just up and let me be.

...Oh, I'm so confused, I don't know what to think.
Are they my friends, or do they once again want to see me sink?
This toxic relationship I've got going on inside,
Sometimes I just want to run away and hide.

I no longer know what is real anymore,
Sometimes I feel like I'm on track, but then I'm not so sure.
Where are all these feelings coming from?
I was certain that for a time, I'd made myself numb.

But now they're back, and I don't know what to do.
Who's going to help me through, this time.....who?
Do others notice these vibes I give out?
Are they just too polite to cut me off?

I've tried to get myself some help, I've really tried.
But how much longer am I to stay on this ride?
The pills and the alcohol, they helped for a while,
But then I figured others were beginning to see through my smile.

Casual relationships, became the route I opted to take,
Just to have another human present, for comfort sake.
But when that too, had run its course,
I was left with the feeling that I hadn't gained as much as I had lost.

So alone again, I chose to remain,
It was my responsibility to handle my pain.
But how much of this can one person take,
Before they reach the point at which they finally break?

A conscious decision needed to be made,
And for that, some of my old ways I had to trade.
It wasn't easy, this much was true,
But it was something I knew I had to do.

So I talked to these voices and we made a deal,
The time had come for me to heal.
And I was not going to let them, control this game,
I was fighting back, things weren't going to be the same.

I look for the good in every situation now,
It was hard work, but I finally taught myself how.
Appreciation for the things I had once taken for granted,
Were now in my mind, firmly planted.

You see, I wasn't about to just give up,
When there was so much out there, how could I stop?
Life is precious and way too short,
To be bogged down by all these negative thoughts.

Through prayer and good friends, I've now found my way,
A price I can never begin to repay.
For too long I've chosen to put myself last,
And chance after chance, I'd just let them pass.

But now I'm done with just standing behind,
It's time for me to get to the front of the line.
No more opportunities are going to pass me by,
To this new and improved me, you better say "Hi".

Because this time I'm ready and I'm here to stay,
And I won't be put down by what anyone has to say.
We all have a past, and from it we can break free.
If ever you doubt yourself, just take a look at me.

I'm a whole new person, with visions and dreams,
And don't for a moment, think it's as easy as it seems.
But I'm determined, I'm going to do it this time.
Just look out and see, victory will be mine.

Don't Judge Me

Don't look at me the way you do,
With such scorn in your eyes.
You don't know what it's like to be me,
Doing whatever it takes to get by.

You judge because, you think you're better
Than me; And that's no lie.
But if you knew the struggles I've faced,
Maybe you could understand my cry.

I don't pretend to be a saint,
In fact, that's far from true.
But at least I know my own self-worth,
Though it may not be obvious to you.

The things I do, I do because
It's the only way I know,
To keep my head above the ground,
I've learnt that long ago.

The life I lead, is not the best,
I know that as well as you.
But when you've lived the life, I've lived,
You do what you have to do.

I'm not like you, who've had it all.
Not a day you've been without.
You've never had to disappoint your kids,
As they stared at you with open mouths.

I know you think I've wasted my life,
And I deserve what I've come to.
But you could never begin to understand,
The pains that I've been through.

You frown on these people I consider my friends,
You scuff at this place I call home.
But you don't know how comforting it's been,
To be accepted as one of their own.

These streets have been my sole refuge.
To you, it may not seem fit.
But truer friends I've never known,
Than those I've shared it with.

They've always been around for me.
From them, I have nothing to hide.
And on the day, they took my boys,
These friends were at my side.

We've laughed together and cried together.
With them, I feel so free.
And I've never doubted, for even a while,
That they'll always be there for me.

So, don't you dare turn your nose up at me!
Don't judge what I've come to.
You'll never truly know where I've been,
Until you've walked a day in my shoe.

Destitution

Tears stream down her pain streaked face,
As she looks for a place to rest her head.
She's tired and cold, and her feet are both sore,
And she's thinking, 'she'd rather be dead'.

If only there was a place she could go,
Where for her there'll be no more sorrow.
A place where she could forget all her past,
And look for a brighter tomorrow.

She never thought she could feel so alone,
With not even one friend in the world.
How could life be so cruel? She wonders,
As she sits in the bitter cold.

People pass and they stare, and they turn up their nose,
When they see her worn out attire.
Never once thinking that maybe she tried,
Or even had the urge to aspire.

Many times she's tried to turn things around,
But each time to no avail.
So she's resigned herself to a life on the street,
For she believes she's destined to fail.

All she needs, is to hear someone say,
'There's no need for you to cry
For there's someone who cares about you,
And He'll see that you get by'.

Last Night I Cried

Last night I lay awake in bed,
With sleep so far away,
And thought of all the suffering,
In the world today.

So many homeless children,
Roaming the streets at night,
Without a place to call their home,
And no one to hear their plight.

I thought of those who lost their lives,
In such a senseless way,
Young children being gunned down,
Even as they play.

So many feel there is no hope,
No answer to their prayers,
And though they try to mask it all,
They cannot hide their tears.

I lay awake and said a prayer,
For those hurting inside,
Asking the Lord to ease their pain,
As I lay in my bed and cried.

A POSITIVE NOTE

As difficult as life may seem, we must remember that there is always hope. Hope for a better future, hope for an end to the pain, hope that our lifelong dreams will finally come true.

For this hope to take form, we must have faith. One doesn't have to be especially religious or even spiritual, but there is often a belief in a higher power. Someone who watches over us, allowing us to go through our trials in life, as these make us stronger. Someone who is there to pull us back if ever we get too close to the edge of the precipice.

Sometimes, it is that little bit of faith that keeps us going from one day to the next. I would like to offer that hope to everyone out there who believes that they're all alone. Take heart, be brave, you've got this.

Good Morning

Good morning world; what a beautiful day!
Give thanks to God, as you kneel to pray.
The possibilities are endless like the sun's rays,
Take advantage of each moment as you go on your way.

No time for sulking, there's too much to be done.
Let go and be free, allow yourself to have fun.
Sit outside with your coffee and enjoy the rising sun.
There's so much to appreciate before the day is done.

Yesterday's troubles, leave them all behind.
When you least expect it, the solutions you'll find.
So why allow these problems, to control your mind?
They'll work themselves out, as today, you unwind.

There's already too much negativity out there,
Why must we all be living in fear?
This world is ours, of it we must take care.
Opportunities are endless, if you'd just be aware.

So only the best, I wish for one and all.
Hold your head up high today and stand tall.
Though trials, at times, may sometimes make you feel small,
Don't worry, you can pick yourself up, each time you fall.

Our Brother's Keeper

What a wonderful place, this world would be,
If we hold off on judgment of the people we see.
For we know not the trials, that they must endure.
If you look beneath the surface, there's always so much more.

Many walk around with smiles, that hide so much pain.
And deep down inside, they're going insane.
A little sensitivity, is all that it takes.
And you'll be surprised to know, someone's day you can make.

A smile, Or a hug, or a "How are you today?"
Is sometimes all a person, needs to hear you say.
The gesture does not have to be a major one,
But you'll be shocked to see, how much good you have done.

It's true, that we all have our own trials in life,
And battle with our own misfortune and strife.
But stepping a moment, away from your grief,
Can sometimes bring, another poor soul, such relief.

So, make the effort, for someone out there.
And share with them, some of your love and cheer.
The joy you will bring, to a suffering heart,
A memory from which, you will never depart.

Take It All In

Look up it's there!
You just have to be aware.
Open your eyes, you'll see,
Around you there's so much beauty.
Take a look at what's around,
The birds and insects, what a beautiful sound.
Now close your eyes and feel the breeze,
As it washes over you with ease.
A deep breath in and you'll find,
That beauty exists in different kinds.
A gentle word spoken to someone, is all it takes,
And the happiness inside them, you can awake.
Sometimes we just need, to open ourselves up,
And stop fighting so hard, to reach the top.
Enjoy each new day, as if it were the last,
And stop dwelling on things, that clutter your past.
There's too much beauty, in this world to ignore,
You just have to know, what you're looking for.

Hey There Girl

This one's for all the girls out there, who think they're not good enough,
You'd be surprised to see, that you're made up of some real strong stuff.
All those thoughts, that you're not as pretty as the other girls,
And surely guys will never pick you, with all the choices in the world.

You're not smart enough, or that's what you make yourself believe.
But in you, I see potential, that you haven't begun to conceive.
But first you've got to stop putting yourself down,
And stop judging yourself by those around.

You're special, unique, one of a kind.
Another like you, they'll never find.
You brighten up a room, whenever you walk in,
And the love of others, no doubt, you can win.

With a smile and a nod, you can make someone's day,
And you always know just the right thing to say.
You are beautiful, both inside and out,
And this is something, you should never doubt.

Your inner beauty, shines out through your pores,
And radiates, filling the room, with your charm and your poise.
And oh, let's not forget your beautiful mind,
That no doubt, will always be one of a kind.

Intelligence is the new sexy, that's what I believe,
So work that brain girl, show them what you can achieve.
At the end of the day, the makeup and fancy clothes will be removed,
But a permanent mark you've made, once yourself, to the world you can prove.

Don't wait for validation, from those on the outside,
You've got to believe in yourself and hold your head up high.
Choose carefully, who you let into your bubble,
Because not everyone's there for you, some are just there to cause trouble.

Be ambitious, but at the same time show compassion,
You never know the depth of someone else's situation.
Be a role model, to the other girls out there,
That's an important thing we're lacking nowadays, I fear.

Show them that beauty and brains, go hand in hand,
And if you have a shining personality, then you're part of an elite band.
You can make the difference, the potential is there,
So stop putting yourself down, to yourself you must be fair.

I believe that you're destined, for many great things,
To me, you're an angel, just without the wings.
Now go out there and let your light shine,
And with the right attitude and confidence, I know you'll be fine.

The Lord Will See You Through

Although at times we may feel down,
And think we're all alone.
There's always someone very near,
Whom we can call our own.

He dries our eyes and calms our fears,
For he loves us very much.
Just close your eyes and think of Him,
And you will feel his touch.

He takes care of His children,
He'll always be around.
And in the times we need Him most,
He'll never let us down.

God wants us to be happy,
He wants us to be whole.
He's by your side, just trust in Him,
And He will take control.

So don't lose faith in Him,
Even when you're feeling blue.
'Cause in your darkest moments,
The Lord will see you through.

The Comforter

The sun rises in the morning,
As you kneel to pray,
Asking God to walk beside you,
And guide you through the day.

You take on all the challenges,
That come along today,
For as long as God is with you,
Nothing will stand in your way.

He keeps a close eye on you,
As you go along your way,
Bringing joy to those who love you,
And He'll never let you stray.

Be good to those around you,
And a kind word always say.
For the love of God is with you,
And in your heart He'll always stay.

You'll kneel beside your bed tonight,
And once again you'll pray,
Thanking God for all the joys of life,
And the blessings of the day.

From The Heart

I don't think I can take any more,
I'm tired and so much in pain,
No one seems to know how I feel,
It's like I'm going insane

Just then a light shines down, from way up high,
And a soft voice calls out my name,
A gentle hand reaches out to me,
And my world is no longer the same.

I close my eyes and extend my hand,
For I know there's nothing to fear,
I kiss the wind as it brushes my face,
In this place, I haven't a care.

A peaceful feeling comes over me,
My heart's as light as a feather.
I embrace this new found feeling of joy,
I can brave the toughest of weather.

Everything now, just seems so surreal,
The world seems a different place.
A carefree smile now adorns my lips,
As the sun caresses my face.

Not a moment too soon He reached out to me,
For He saw that I needed a friend.
He stood with me when I needed Him most,
And by me He will always stand.

Rewards of Love

Life is full of wonders,
And full of pleasures too,
We may come upon some blunders,
But love will see us through.

Happiness does not cost a penny,
This no doubt is true.
For the gifts from God are many,
Every day there's something new.

The benefits of caring,
Sometimes seem so few,
But the rewards are never ending,
With birds and skies of blue.

As long as there is hope and faith,
Goodness will shine through,
And it will all be worth the wait,
When LOVE comes disguised as you.

Printed in the United States
By Bookmasters